THE · PARENT · AND · CHILD · PROGRAMME ·

More Monster Maths

Ruth Merttens

Senior Lecturer, Maths Education, Polytechnic of North London

Illustrated by Terri Gower

Meet Ram and Rom

Ram

Rom

Rom and Ram are robots. Before you start this book, you need to program them by filling in the scores for their abilities below.

Throw the 2 dice. Multiply the 2 numbers. Then put that number in one of the boxes below. This means that the highest score they can have for each ability is **36** (**6 x 6**) and the lowest is **1** (**1 x 1**).

Abilities

Rom Ram

1 **Speed** – how fast they can walk.

2 **Movement** – how well they can move their arms and legs.

3 **Communication** – how well they can talk and understand.

4 **Cost** – how expensive they are to run.

5 **Solving problems** – how good they are at thinking out answers.

6 **Mechanics** – how good they are at building or making things.

Hint

If you need some help multiplying the numbers, use the tables square on page 19 to help you.

When you have programmed them, work out which robot you would use for the activities below.

Look at the abilities the robots will need for each activity. Add up the scores for these abilities. Write them in the columns on the chart below.

Then write the name of the robot you would use on the chart.

You will need to look at these abilities.

Activities

1	Run a race	1, 2, 4
2	Make a phone call	3, 4
3	Work out a sum and tell you the answer	3, 4, 5
4	Build a bridge	4, 5, 6
5	Bake a cake	2, 4, 6

Activity	Abilities needed	Rom's score	Ram's score	Robot chosen
1				
2				
3				
4				
5				

3

Multiplying grid

You can play this game with a friend or against Rom or Ram.

You will need

2 dice
1 black pen
1 blue pen

Throw the 2 dice. Multiply the 2 numbers. Use a black pen to fill in the answer on the grid in one of the possible spaces.
For example, **2 x 5 = 10**.
Write **10** in the square **2** along and **5** up **or** in the square **5** along and **2** up. You can only write your answer in **one** square, not in both.
Now your friend can throw the 2 dice and do the same thing, using a blue pen. If you are playing against Rom or Ram you can throw for them.

Go on throwing the 2 dice in turn. The first player to get **4** numbers in a line in any direction is the winner.

x	1	2	3	4	5	6
6						
5						
4						
3						
2						
1						

Hint
When you have filled in all the numbers you can play the game again by using 2 different coloured counters to cover the numbers as you play.

Over the moon

When a number goes over the moon, something happens to it. Can you work out what it is and use the same rule to fill in the empty boxes in this chart?

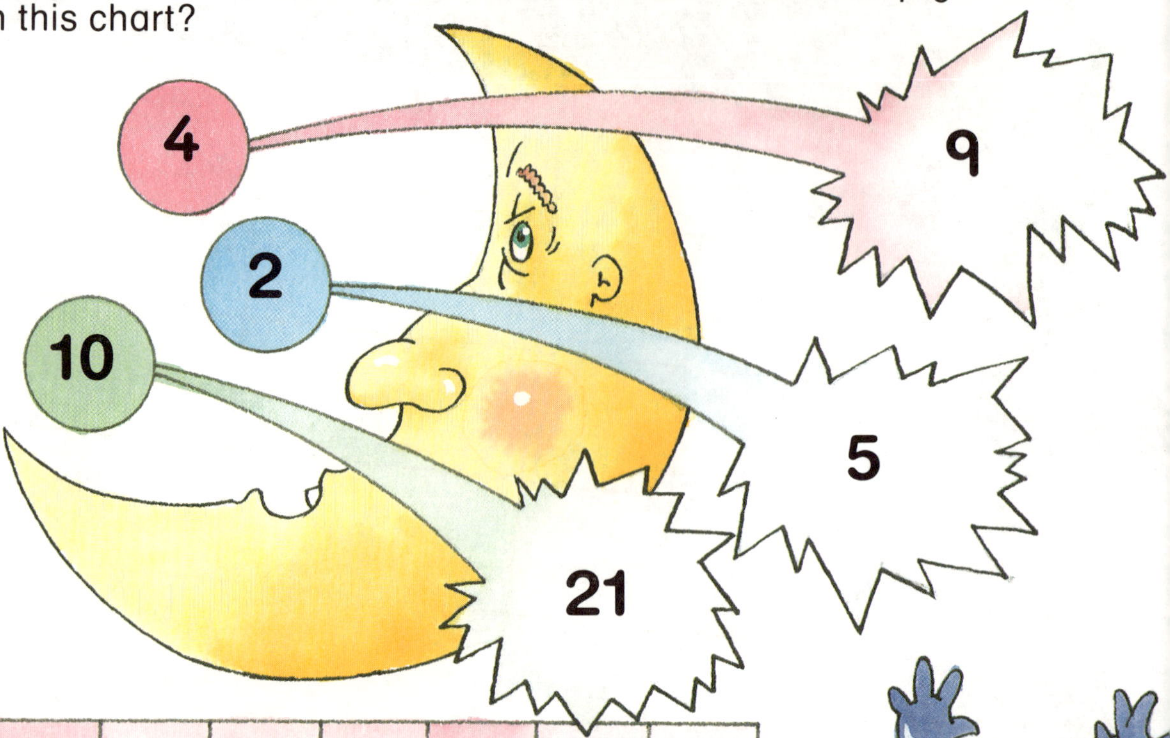

4

2

10

9

5

21

1	9	3	7	5	8	11	6
↓	↓	↓	↓	↓	↓	↓	↓
3							

When a number goes over the rainbow, a different thing happens to it. Can you work out what it is and use the same rule to fill in the empty boxes here?

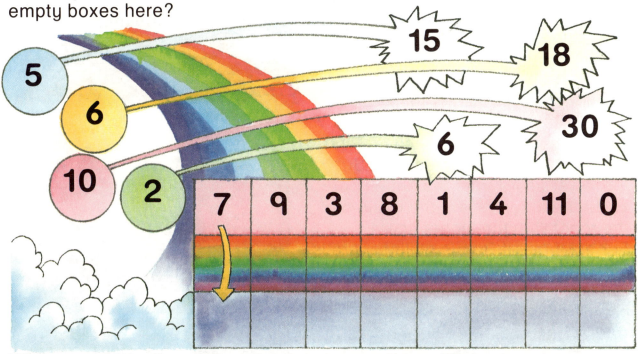

When a number goes over this planet, something different again happens. Can you work out what it is and use the same rule to fill in the empty boxes?

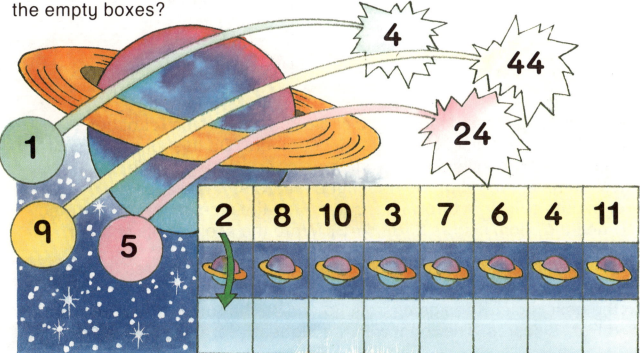

Robot race

Ram and Rom are taking part in an obstacle race. To help them you will need 2 dice and 2 counters.

They start on the first square. The number tells you which ability they will need to build a tall brick tower. Now look at their scores on page 2. Subtract the lower score from the higher score. Write the difference in the column of the robot with the higher score. For example, if Rom's ability score is **30** and Ram's is **12**, Rom scores **18** (**30−12=18**). Write the score in her column.

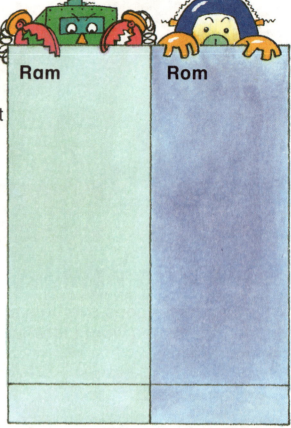

Ram	Rom

Total

Now Rom and Ram move on to a circle. Choose which robot goes first. Throw the 2 dice. Multiply the 2 numbers. Do this for each robot and subtract the lower score from the higher. Write the difference in the column of the robot with the higher score on the dice. For example, if Ram throws a **2** and a **4** on the dice, and Rom throws a **1** and a **6**, Ram scores **2** (**8−6=2**). Write the score in his column.

Then the robots move on to the next square. Find the scores for the abilities needed and do as you did for the first square. Then move on to the next circle. Keep going until you finish the race. Add up Rom's and Ram's scores. The robot with the highest score has won.

Circle areas

Ram is working out the **area** of this circle. Can you help him? The area is the number of squares a shape covers. To make it easier to count the squares, he has drawn a big square inside the circle.

He counts the number of squares along one side of the big square. $\boxed{11}$

Then he multiplies this number by itself to find the total number of squares in the big square. $\boxed{11} \times \boxed{11} = \boxed{121}$

Next he counts the number of squares outside the big square. He counts any squares that are **more than half** and leaves out squares which are **less than half.**

Write down the number of squares outside the big square. $\boxed{}$

Now add the 2 totals together. $\boxed{121} + \boxed{} = \boxed{}$

The area of the circle = $\boxed{}$ squares.

Now draw your own circle in the space below.
You could use a cup to draw around.

Draw a big square in the middle of the circle.

Count the squares along one side of it. ☐

Then multiply this number by itself to find the number of squares in the big square. You may need to use a calculator. ☐

Count the squares around the edge of the big square. ☐

Add the **2** totals together to find the area. ☐

Monster number chains

How to make a number chain

Find a piece of paper and a pencil.
Think of a number. Write it down and draw a circle round it.
Then use your calculator to follow these rules.

If your number is even, halve it.

If it is odd, multiply it by **3** and add **1**.

Write down the answers in a chain like the monster's one.

Start

11

$11 \times 3 = 33^{+1} =$

34

$34 \div 2 =$

17

$17 \times 3 = 51^{+1} =$

52

26

13

40

Now look at the bottom of the monster's chain. Did the same thing happen at the end of your chain? Did you find that the numbers kept repeating and you could go no further?

Try another number. Did the same thing happen?

Which numbers work fast?
Which numbers work slowly?

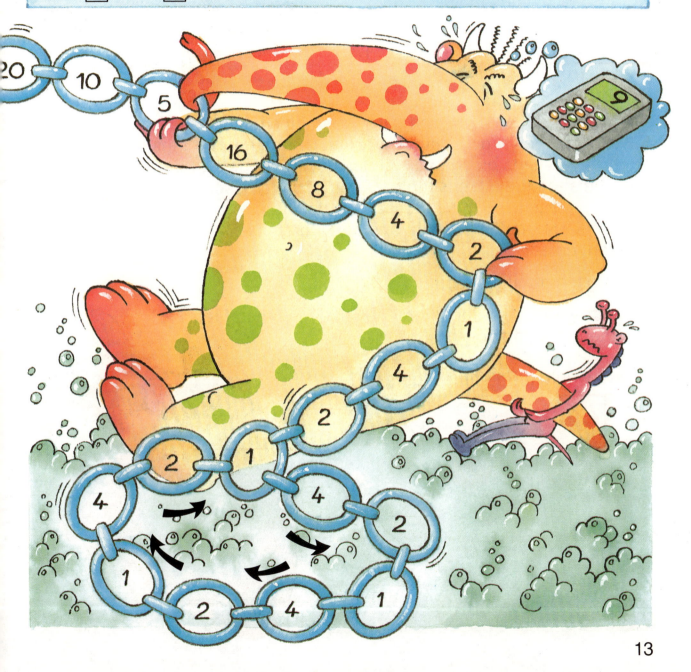

Tables graph

Here is the **5** times table.

1	2	3	4	5	6	7	8	9	10	11	12
5	10	15	20	25	30	35	40	45	50	55	60

You can draw it on the graph. Draw a small cross ✗ **1** line along and **5** lines up. Then draw another ✗ **2** lines along and **10** lines up. Draw another ✗ **3** lines along and **15** lines up. Go on doing this until you have finished the **5** times table. Some of the crosses have been drawn in for you. Join the crosses with a line.

Write out another times table and plot it on your graph using a different colour.

Now try a third times table.

What do you notice about the lines in each times table?
Are they always straight?

Where would the **13** times table go?

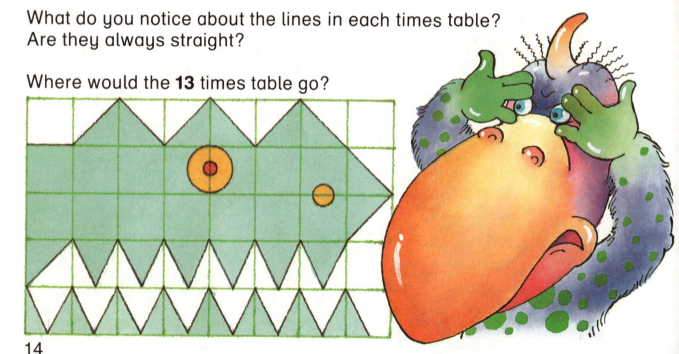

14

15

Fraction wall

Look at this fraction wall.

You can build one too. Here is how.

Draw **one** line of **24** squares at the bottom of the space below. Colour in the squares. Draw a **2nd** line of **24** squares on top. Colour it. Divide it into **2** equal pieces. Draw a **3rd** line on top. Colour it. Divide it into **4** equal pieces. Draw a **4th** line on top. Divide it into **8** equal pieces.

Look at your fraction wall.
How many squares are there in each **half** of the **2nd** row up? _____

How many squares are there in each **quarter** of the **3rd** row up? _____

How many **quarters** are there in that row? _____

The top row is in **eighths.**

How many **eighths** are there in that row? _____

How many squares are there in each **eighth**? _____

How many **quarters** sit on one **half**? _____

How many **eighths** do you need to make one **half**? _____

Now answer these sums.

24 ÷ 2 =

24 ÷ 8 =

24 ÷ 3 =

24 ÷ 6 =

24 ÷ 4 =

Tables picture

A picture of one of Rom's friends is hidden in this oblong. Can you help her find him? Here is how.

First, colour all the numbers in the **7** times table.
Second, colour all the numbers in the **5** times table.
Third, colour all the numbers in the **9** times table.
Finally, colour all the numbers in the **8** times table.
Use a different colour for each times table.

12	6	17	31	3	25	40	10	12	19	31
2	4	13	2	39	49	50	28	34	13	26
34	11	57	4	61	5	56	35	2	46	43
19	47	33	53	29	51	45	1	39	29	22
22	41	21	49	8	64	16	64	48	49	38
23	38	28	44	16	48	24	32	8	21	11
59	3	77	31	48	16	32	8	32	28	37
63	14	7	47	24	32	8	64	16	77	23
17	57	11	59	32	16	24	48	8	7	12
6	26	67	41	64	8	16	32	48	14	17
33	1	57	62	9	91	31	13	9	63	7
19	66	13	79	81	41	34	51	81	13	41
37	12	53	69	18	83	26	44	18	1	6
2	58	83	36	27	2	11	36	27	22	12
62	11	23	54	72	43	79	54	72	37	2
4	61	67	9	81	12	3	81	9	53	19
43	49	58	36	54	49	17	36	54	33	46
17	14	56	7	28	28	7	56	14	58	2

Use this tables square to help you.

1	2	3	4	5	6	7	8	9	10
2	4	6	8	10	12	14	16	18	20
3	6	9	12	15	18	21	24	27	30
4	8	12	16	20	24	28	32	36	40
5	10	15	20	25	30	35	40	45	50
6	12	18	24	30	36	42	48	54	60
7	14	21	28	35	42	49	56	63	70
8	16	24	32	40	48	56	64	72	80
9	18	27	36	45	54	63	72	81	90
10	20	30	40	50	60	70	80	90	100

Monster invasion

The Earth is being invaded by monsters. These monsters are very powerful! They can double their number every hour!

If only **one** monster arrives on Earth, can you work out how many hours it will take until there are too many monsters for the number to fit on your calculator? Here is how.

Press the number **1** on your calculator. Then double it by pressing **×** **2** **=** .

Do this again. How many times can you double the number until it gets too big for the screen and an **E** appears?

There is a quick way to make your calculator do something such as multiply by **2** again and again. Press **2**, then **×** **2** **=** and then **=** again. With some calculators you may have to press **2** **×** **×** **2** **=** instead. Try it out!

How many monsters will there be after a day and a half?

Hint

There are **24** hours in a day.

Try to find out how many hours it would take for the number of monsters to reach **1,000,000** – one million!

Day of birth

You can use your calculator to work out the **day** you were born like this.

Ram's example

1. Take the last two figures of the year in which you were born.

$1979 \rightarrow 79$

2. Divide by **12**.

$79 \div 12 =$ and   6
7 over

3. Divide the number left over by **4**.

$7 \div 4 =$ 1   3 over

4. Write down the **date** of the month you were born on. (Ram was born on September **12**.) Add up the **4** numbers in the orange column.

12

26

5. Add the right number for your month. Ram adds **6**

6

January	**1**	April	**2**	July	**0**	October	**1**
February	**4**	May	**2**	August	**3**	November	**4**
March	**4**	June	**5**	September	**6**	December	**6**

(If you were born in January or February of a leap year, subtract **1**.)

32

6. Divide by **7**. What is left over?

$32 \div 7 = 4$
and **4** over.

7. Look at the number in the red box and match it to a day.

| Saturday | **0** | Monday | **2** | Wednesday | **4** | Friday | **6** |
| Sunday | **1** | Tuesday | **3** | Thursday | **5** | | |

Ram was born on a Wednesday.

Ask as many of your friends and family as possible for their date of birth. Work out the day they were born on and write it down.
Then colour a block above that day on the graph.
Collect as many days as you can to make a good graph.

people	Monday	Tuesday	Wednesday	Thursday	Friday	Saturday	Sunday
6							
5							
4							
3							
2							
1							

Day of birth

More about this book

The maths workbooks in **The Parent and Child Programme** are an extension of the activity books. The exercises and games in this workbook reinforce and practise skills covered in the activity book, **Maths with Monsters.**

Enjoy it! Children enjoy doing things with a parent. Working together allows children to talk about what they are doing and to put things into their own words. This is a vital part of the learning process. Sharing the experience of learning not only helps the child but also makes learning thoroughly enjoyable.

There is no danger of conflicting with school work; the activities in this book have been carefully chosen to fit in with the maths schemes used in schools. If an activity is proving too difficult or the child becomes tired, leave it until another time. Never try to do too much at once. This book contains a variety of activities and inevitably each child will find some more stimulating than others.

The importance of understanding: there is now a strong emphasis in maths teaching to encourage children to develop their own methods for doing things so that they are always very clear about what they are doing and why it works. By working in this way, children become more able to relate skills learnt in the classroom to situations in everyday life. All the paper and pencil calculations in the world are no use if the only place that the child can do them is in the maths lesson at school and in their maths book! Sums are only useful if children understand them and can use them in other situations.

Tables: teachers, parents and children themselves, want children to know their tables! The question is how to achieve this. The most helpful way for children to practise their tables is in a variety of different situations and in a number of different ways. It is **much more effective** to do a small amount of tables practice — say 5 minutes — daily, than to do an hour once a week. It is also particularly helpful if skills like these can be practised in a context where they make sense, in the course of a game, for example, or in order to work out something while shopping.

Calculators play an increasingly important role as children progress in maths. Their use does **not** mean that the children do not have to learn number facts. Rather, calculators give them an opportunity to do calculations using those number facts, to experiment with and investigate the relationships between numbers, and to develop a thorough understanding of the maths involved in some of the number operations. Encouraging children to play with a calculator, to try things out, and to check their answers and test their predictions, plays a critical part in successful maths education today.